Clinton Scollard

Hills of Song

Clinton Scollard

Hills of Song

ISBN/EAN: 9783743305205

Manufactured in Europe, USA, Canada, Australia, Japa

Cover: Foto ©ninafisch / pixelio.de

Manufactured and distributed by brebook publishing software (www.brebook.com)

Clinton Scollard

Hills of Song

TABLE OF CONTENTS

	Page
Taillefer the Trouvère	1
The Blue Arras	4
Sunrise on the Alps	7
My May	9
The Seekers	10
The Walk	12
The Fairies' Pool	13
Sea-fog	14
The Old Desire	15
The Comrades	16
On the Edge of the Woods	17
The Old Gate-keeper	18
By the Stream at Sunset	19
The Mariner's Grave	21
The Dormant Strain	21
The By-path	22
The Sexton	24
The Violet Bank	25
The Crickets by Lake Huron	26
Wild Plum	27
A Bell	28
IN ITALIA	
The Shepherd of the Liro	33
Memories of Como	34
Nuova Luna	35
The Phantom Gondolier	37
A Venetian Sunset	39
On a Copy of Theocritus	40
The Falling of the Burrs	42
A Florentine Garden	43
The Bells of Fossombrone	45

Ex Oriente
Al Mamoun — 51
Dawn in the Desert — 53
Karoon, the Pilgrim — 54
Hassan's Tomb — 56
The Rose of Fayûm — 57
The Dervish's Prayer — 58
At the Funeral of Abdallah — 59
The Vengeance of Kafur — 61
The Arab's Horse — 64
In a Bazaar — 66
Christmas at Marsaba — 68
From an Eastern Oriel — 74

Madrigals
Vive la Bagatelle — 79
The Sweet o' the Year — 80
A Cavalier's Valentine — 82
With Some White Hyacinths in Winter — 83
Ingle Song — 84
Be Ye in Love with April-tide — 85
A Spring Glee — 86
Roses of June — 87
Strawberries — 87
A Summer Song — 88
Wild Thyme — 89
The Even-Song — 90
A Perfect Day — 91
The Bowers of Paradise — 92
Holly Song — 92

TAILLEFER THE TROUVÈRE

THEY sailed in their long gray galleys, they tossed on the narrow sea,
Till dim in the mists of morning were the shores of Normandy.
They were sixty thousand warriors, with never a fear at heart;
They were knights and squires and yeomen, adept in the soldier's art;
They were knights and squires and yeomen, whose school was the press of men,
Whose alphabet was their armor, whose sword was their only pen;
And none of the bold war-farers, though the flower of the land was there,
Bared braver brow to the south wind than Taillefer the Trouvère.

No laugh like his at the banquet, no hand like his on the lute,
No voice like his in the courtyard to banter the brawlers mute;
And never from lip of a jester did a blither quip take wing,
And never on caitiff's cuirass did a nobler brand outring.
But song was the soul of his living; aye! song was the breath of his life;
He had taken song to brother, he had taken song to wife.

THE HILLS OF SONG

In the tide-pulse of the ocean, in the wild wind-pulse of air,
There was more than mortal music to Taillefer the Trouvère.

They have harried the coast of Sussex, they have harried the coast of Kent;
They have trod the soil of the Saxon, and come to his peakèd tent,—
To the fortressed hill of Senlac, that out of a marsh uprears,
Where the golden Wessex dragon is hedged by the gleam of spears.
They have girt them tight for the onset, they have leaped in line for the fray;
What manner of man shall lead them, shall show them the victor's way?
To be first to fall on a foeman what manner of man shall dare?
Neither valorous knight nor bowman, but Taillefer the Trouvère.

In front of the foremost footman he spurs with a clarion cry,
And raises the song of Roland to the apse of the glowing sky.
A moment the autumn's glory is a joy to the singer's sight,
And the war-lay soars the stronger, like a falcon, up the height;

TAILLEFER THE TROUVÈRE.

Then springs there a Saxon hus-carl, with thews
   like the forest oak,
And, whirling a brand of battle, he launches a
   titan stroke;
A sudden and awful shadow, a blot on the azure
   glare,
And dawn in a world unbordered for Taillefer
   the Trouvère.

Shall song overspan the ages for the Duke men
   name the Great,
Who founded the walls of empire on the ruins
   of a state?
Nay! not unto him our greeting across the flood
   of the years,
With the countless slain ensanguined, and bitter
   with mourners' tears;
But unto the soul of the singer, to him of the
   fearless heart,
Shall our hail-cry strengthen starward o'er the
   seas that have no chart;
For song was the love of his lifetime, and he met
   death's chill eclipse
On the verge of the fight at Senlac with a song
   upon his lips.

THE HILLS OF SONG

THE BLUE ARRAS

'Twas the night of a bitter frost
   In the vale of the Bishop's Praise,
And the face of the moon was lost
   In the white of a spectral haze.

The voice of the wind was whist
   Where the Hall hung over the lake;
But the logs on the fire-dogs hissed
   Like a serpent roused in a brake.

Rich were the walls of the room
   With the trophies of wealth and fame;
But the Bishop cowered in the gloom
   Aback from the searching flame.

Never an eye he cast
   On all that the years had won;
But he shrunk from the sight, aghast
   At a deed that was like to be done.

Though it stung his touch like a thorn,
   At a tiny scrip clutched he
That read, "Come thou at the morn,
   Or I die on the gallows-tree!"

THE BLUE ARRAS

And the sign that was set thereto
  Was his only brother's sign.
The sputtering flame burned blue,
  And the deer-hound gave a whine,

But still did the Bishop brood
  As the moments sped amain,
And his o'erwrought outer mood
  Showed the battle within his brain.

"Tarry!" the Tempter cried;
  "Why save what has little worth?
'T were better that such should bide
  Under five warm feet of earth!

"When rancor and strife are rife,
  Forsooth, 't were a foolish thing
To rescue the worthless life
  Of a rebel against the King!

"His leagues of land shall be thine
  From the plain to the eagle-perch,
And brighter thy name shall shine
  On the brow of the Mother Church."

Then, born of an old desire,
  The Bishop saw, as he sat,
Take form in the core of the fire
  The red of a cardinal's hat.

THE HILLS OF SONG

So he said to his soul, "'T is done!"
  And it seemed, for a breathing space,
That the Tempter's words had won,
  By the look on the Bishop's face.

But sudden the flame shot up
  Till it set the room ashine
Like the bowl of a crystal cup
  Aflood with the gold of wine.

And the hangings, one and all,
  The marvel of Artois skill,
Wavered upon the wall
  Like boughs when the wind hath will.

Wrought on a blue as bland
  As the softest sky of spring,
At the Bishop's own command,
  There was many a sacred thing.

All of the saints most fair
  Who had fought for the faith and bled,
From Jesus, the Christ, were there,
  With a halo about the head.

And lo! as the Bishop gazed,
  With the firelight still at flood,
Each raptured face grew hazed
  With a blurring mist of blood.

SUNRISE ON THE ALPS

But every eye was clear
   And burned like a living coal,
While the wrathful rays pierced sheer
   To the depths of the Bishop's soul;

And each thin lip seemed to frame
   A word that stabbed like a blade;
For he thought it the hated name
   Of him who the Christ betrayed.

Froze in his throat the prayer
   So glib on his tongue before,
And down from his carven chair
   Slipped the Bishop upon the floor;

Groveled,— abashed, abased,—
   Shorn of each shred of pride;
And he lay there, downward-faced,
   Till the glowing firelight died.

But when, with their clear "God-speed,"
   Rang the bells to the day new-born,
Astride of his swiftest steed
   Rode the Bishop to meet the morn.

SUNRISE ON THE ALPS

HARK! how the wakened echoes ring!
   The blaring of the Alpine horn
From peak to peak goes quavering

THE HILLS OF SONG

Through all the slumbering isles of morn.
The first faint line of sunrise fire
  Along the cloudy east is drawn,
And one by one the stars expire
  As rings the anthem-peal of dawn.

Come forth! and taste the winy air
  While yet the dews are opal-bright;
Come forth! and speed with thankful prayer
  The shadow of the wings of night;
Come forth! and watch the unsullied snows,
  Range after lofty range, expand;
Come forth! and see the morning's rose
  Burst o'er the Bernese Oberland.

Swift-smitten by a transient ray,
  A lordly pinnacle of ice
Becomes, in some mysterious way,
  A giant spray of edelweiss;
And on the horizon's utmost bound
  From peak to cloud one may espy,
Round rising over rainbow round,
  A Jacob's-ladder scale the sky.

The west has felt a flush of flame
  That sets its forest heart astir,
And breathes the radiant morning's name
  In symphonies of pine and fir.
The lower mists are backward rolled,
  And, as the crowning splendors burn,

MY MAY

    They kindle into lambent gold
        The blue enamel of Lucerne.

Now every heaven-aspiring height,
    From mountain pole to mountain pole,
Reveals to the enraptured sight
    Its evanescent aureole.
The scars the breast of nature wore
    Are thrown in such divine eclipse,
The soul of man is dumb before
    The dawn's supreme apocalypse.

MY MAY

HARK to the joyful sound ! to the revel of rills !
The buds have leaped into leaf on a thousand hills ;
The only snow is the snow of the orchard spray ;
She cometh across the land, my May, my May !

There springeth a fire at the root of growing things ;
There stirreth desire at the heart that awakes and sings ;
The breast of the blue is shot with a brighter ray ;
She cometh across the land, my May, my May !

THE HILLS OF SONG

She cometh with kindling eyes and with morning
  smiles,
O'er the sapphire-shining seas from the golden
  isles;
Her breath is that of the jasmine bloom and the
  bay;
She cometh across the land, my May, my May!

She quickeneth drowsing hope by her calm
  caress;
She bringeth us heart-content for a balm to bless;
O, to lure her feet awhile from the June-ward
  way!
She cometh across the land, my May, my May!

But enough! She cometh. Rejoice, my soul,
  rejoice!
Join, O my voice, with the universal voice,
To hail the dream-delight of her dream-brief
  stay!
She cometh across the land, my May, my May!

THE SEEKERS

FRIEND, I pray thee, who be they
  That do roam adown the day
With such lorn and lifeless stride,
Wan of face and weary-eyed?
Ho! ye wanderers pinched and pale,

THE SEEKERS

On what long unbeaten trail
Go ye? — on what unknown quest?

>   *Thus the hapless ones confessed,* —
>   *" Seek we east, and seek we west,*
>   *For the sacred chrism of rest."*

" Hold," the curious questioner said,
" For a space thy toilsome tread :
Haply nearer than ye dream
Is the balm ye so esteem ! "
Then upon him full they turned
Eyes in whose dull embers burned
Longing, as a sleepless guest.

>   *" Ah ! " they sighed, " then were we blest,*
>   *Seeking east, and seeking west,*
>   *For the sacred chrism of rest."*

" I," the questioner said, " will guide
To the boon so sanctified ;
Follow me, and ye shall see
Where the haunts of heart's-ease be ! "
Wotted then the seekers well
'T was the angel Azrael,
And they bowed at his behest.

>   *" Aye ! " they answered, " it is best !*
>   *Seeking east, and seeking west,*
>   *We have found the chrism of rest."*

THE HILLS OF SONG

THE WALK

I WOULD go forth among the hills
  The green, crest-climbing lane along,
For now the cup that morning fills
  Is brimmed with light and song.

And I would hail as "comrade mine"
  Each soul soe'er that seeks and sees
The overtures of One divine
  In dawn's antiphonies.

Up shall we mount until we find
  The pinnacle of prospect won,
And see the sinuous stream unwind
  Its silver in the sun.

Our spirits, purified of haste,
  By dews of freedom cleansed of care,
Shall laugh, and leap anew, to taste
  The largess of the air.

The wide outreachings of our sight
  Yon purple ridges shall not bind,
But only some Andean height
  Horizoning the mind.

THE FAIRIES' POOL

By radiant apotheosis
    To Eden earth shall seem re-born:
So shall we find the chrism of bliss
    Upon the hills of morn.

THE FAIRIES' POOL

OVERHEAD, the maple branches mingle,
    Sigh and sough in breezes ever cool;
Underneath, where dips the darkling dingle,
    Lies that liquid glass, the fairies' pool.

Rare the ray that lights its brooding beryl —
    Sunshine, moonshine, or the starshine pale;
And its dusky depths seem paved with peril
    To the wanderer in that lonely vale.

There's a legend that the white leaves whisper —
    Poplar, birch, and aspen, softly blown —
That from spring till autumn airs grow crisper
    Water fairies hold it for their own.

Such a brood as in our dreams beguile us,
    Visions of dead Arcady re-born,
Kin to that bewitching shape that Hylas
    Followed down to death one golden morn.

Fain were I to let the legend linger,
    Not to dagger its frail life with fact,

THE HILLS OF SONG

Though the real lift a scornful finger,
    Cry — " Romance is but a barren tract ! "

Should the singer turn his back on beauty ?
    May there not be meaning in a myth ?
Is it now the poet's highest duty
    But to aim at pungency and pith ?

Shall we clip the mounting wings of fancy,
    And imagination rein by rule ?
Nay ! I hail the olden necromancy ! —
    This wood-mirror is the fairies' pool.

SEA-FOG

OUT of the sensuous sunlands of the south
    On wings of gold a lustrous spirit came,
The smile of summer lingering round her mouth,
    Her languorous eyes noon-fervent as with flame.

Out from the pallid aisleways of the pole
    A somber spirit sped adown the sea ;
Snow-raimented as is the shrivèd soul,
    Wan-browed and weird and spectre-like was he.

Somewhere upon the landless void these twain,
    In that dim, dateless æon of the dead,
Met as they moved above the mighty main,
    Loved with immortal rapture, and were wed.

THE OLD DESIRE

From this strange union was one daughter born,
 A lithe, elusive **creature,** evermore
Blinding the stars, bewildering the morn,
 And winging like a wraith from shore to shore.

With the soft, white persuasion of her lips
 More to be feared than all the **sirens** she ;
Snared by her spells, how many stately ships
 Will sail no more the blue paths of the sea !

THE OLD DESIRE

THERE kindles within **my** breast
 Ever **the** old desire,
When wavers along the **west**
 The maple's beacon-fire.

It's oh ! **to be out on** the hills
 Over the **dead, dull** plain,
To hear the autumn rills
 Echo the far refrain ;

To pluck the milkweed's down
 From its prison within the pod,
And mint the gold for a crown
 From the ore of the golden-rod ;

To taste **the oil** of the nut
 That **is racy** ripe **at the core,**

THE HILLS OF SONG

And the tang in the flag root shut
    By the singing rillet's shore;

To drain from the bounteous cruse
    The purple wine of delight,
To dream the feet of the Muse
    Are twinkling along the height;

To gather all gracious gain
    In sight, in scent, and in song,
Against the ruin of rain,
    And the winter white and long.

I see it along the west,
    The maple's beacon-fire,
And there kindles within my breast
    Ever the old desire.

THE COMRADES

ALONG the highways of the year,
    The only paths that have no end,
Two comrades, tried and true and dear,
    Go hand in hand as friend with friend.

Indifferent are they if the dawn
    Withholds its crimson, or the noon,
Behind a veil of grey withdrawn,
    Denies its amber for a boon.

ON THE EDGE OF THE WOODS

The rain may scurry up the glade,
  And blur the sunset's brilliant book,
Their faces in the twilight shade
  Will ever wear the rainbow look.

All life to them is light and large
  With summit prospects, if they stray
By sere December's rimy marge,
  Or by the bloomy shores of May.

From dales of doubt and peaks of care
  No woe-winds blow with chill annoy;
They walk in earth's diviner air,
  These comrades leal, Content and Joy.

ON THE EDGE OF THE WOODS

MIDWAY between the glare and gloom
  In this cool twilight let us lie;
Around, a fringe of golden bloom,
  Above, an arch of leafy sky,
  And breezes blowing blandly by.

List to the wood-choir's swelling praise!
  The hermit-thrush is chorister:
Down all the deep and dusky ways
  The choral melodies concur
  With soft profundos from the fir.

THE HILLS OF SONG

If, where the sunlight dints the shade
  With amber dimples, some astray
Four-footed thing our view invade,
  Although it perk and whisk away,
  No discord jars the rhythmic day.

Here all is harmony, and here
  Care, garment-like, is cast aside;
Ours is the vision of the seer;
  And, since our dearest dreams abide,
  The yearning soul is satisfied.

THE OLD GATE-KEEPER

As you turned from the town, and the valley forsook,
Lured onward and up by the brawl of a brook,
There broke on the sight such a tiny abode,
The gate-house that stood at the bend in the road.

Long, long to the hill with its sheltering breast
It had cuddled as close as a bird to its nest;
And never came night but its window-panes glowed
With a welcome flung out at the bend in the road.

The quaintest of mortals had lodging therein,
With the dream of a dimple asleep in his chin;
And a bow like a prince which he fondly bestowed
When he flung wide the gate at the bend in the road.

BY THE STREAM AT SUNSET

Though his stock was askew and his wig was **awry**,
The laugh and the lustre that leaped from his eye
Told his heart held the love of his kind for its code,
The odd little man at the bend in the road.

He would brood by the hour o'er his **one** window-box,
With its old-fashioned blossoms, **sweet**-william and phlox,
Yet the cloud always fled, and the mirth ever flowed,
When a wanderer paused at the bend in the road.

His life had its story, 't was whispered, and woe
Had crushed the fair flower of his hopes at a blow;
And yet to the last he made light of his load,
The brave little **man at** the bend in the road.

Now he sleeps his last sleep, though in **memory** still
I see his bent figure lean over the sill;
And gone is the gate-house, his cheery abode,
While the grass waves its green at the bend in the **road.**

BY THE STREAM AT SUNSET

I HAVE come, O, I have come
The thronged hot highways **from,**
And found me a bowery nook

THE HILLS OF SONG

By a tranquil-breasted brook,
Where there's not a voice to mourn
That the day is nigh out-worn.

I can filch the gold of rest
From the embers in the west,
And can spin my dreams as fine
As the wild cucumber vine
With its snowy fluff of flower;
I can fashion thews of power
From the oak tree, rooted stanch,
And my hope-boats I can launch
With the bubbles that drift and swirl
Where the brown sands shade to pearl.
I can make my purpose gleam
Like the bronze stems in mid-stream;
My fancies I can shape
Like the tendrils of the grape;
I can harbor thoughts as fair
As the white spiræ there,
That lifts not a look of scorn
To its big rough neighbor thorn.

'T is hence, O, hence I have come
The thronged hot highways from,
That the healing power may work
Through the lethargy and murk
Of the mind, and there inspire
The old chords of desire, —
The pure desire that leads
To the goal of lofty deeds.

THE MARINER'S GRAVE

THE MARINER'S GRAVE

BENEATH the grim old beacon tower
  They made his last straight bed,
The gray and grizzled slope below,
  And ocean wide outspread.

There might he see the ships slip in
  And out across the bar,
And down the night the warning light
  Fling its recurrent star.

There might he hear the harping wind
  Retune its ancient strain,
And that sublime musician, sea,
  Intone its joy and pain.

There might his sleep be long and deep,
  From time and tide withdrawn;
Above, the sea-gull's silvery wing
  Until the last red dawn.

THE DORMANT STRAIN

SOMETIMES there stirs a dormant strain
  Of woodland blood within my vein,
And scorn of custom and of art
Lays heavy hold upon my heart.

THE HILLS OF SONG

The garden, with its ordered rows,
To me no line of beauty shows;
I long for nature unconfined,
Unmanacled, as is the wind.

Then plunge I deep in dales where rills
Come hurrying downward from the hills,
Where briar and berry intertwine,
And pungent odors breathes the pine;
Where banks are velveted with moss,
And wild-grape tendrils climb and cross
From bough to bough, and mandrake fruit
Is plenty by the beech tree's root.

You, in the city hived and shut,
Here is the kernel of life's nut! —
To feel the savage in you stir,
To know yourself a wanderer
In haunts where wilding things have birth,
To taste the freshness of the earth, —
Its balm, its myrrh, — for once to scan
The virile primal joys of man.

THE BY-PATH

UP through the whispering grove it winds,
  And on through woodland cloisters fair,
Where, hid in hollows deep, one finds
  The shy and slender maiden-hair.

THE BY-PATH

On this side hazel copses reach ;
   On that, long shadowy aisles unroll,
Propt by the granite of the beech
   And the white birch's marble bole.

Hither, when spring was in the bud,
   I saw two laughing lovers stray ;
June leaped within his nimble blood,
   And in her eyes there brooded May.

To them the world was sweet with song,
   And myths were care and gray regret ;
They plucked, the while they strolled along,
   The morn-empurpled violet.

Once more I saw the lovers pass,
   Grown tender and less mirthful now ;
The breeze sang "summer" through the grass,
   And "summer" through the full-leaved bough.

I wandered through the wood again
   When autumn spread her crimson spell,
But saw them not, for o'er the plain
   Out pealed their silvern wedding-bell.

And after those Elysian days
   No more they trod the pleasant path,
But wended down life's wider ways
   To gather love's full aftermath.

THE HILLS OF SONG

And yet whene'er I seek the place
  I feel their living presence there;
Still, still abide her bloom and grace,
  And lingers still his rapturous air.

The seasons turn from green to sere,
  And petty cares and discords move,
But one spot keeps through all the year
  A perpetuity of love.

THE SEXTON

I WANDERED lone within a churchyard old,
  Amid the lichened tombs, whereon were traced,
In fading characters, the names of those
Who erst were busy upon earthly ways.
The summer wind among the sycamores
Breathed solemn requiem. On the gray church walls
One spreading spray of ivy heralded
The crimson sunsets of autumnal eves.
Across the sward, threading a sinuous way
Between the sunken mounds, the sexton came
Slowly, with shambling gait, his knees ashake.
His grizzled beard hung like a fringe of rime
Upon his ashen cheeks; his wrinkled brow
Was like a parchment written on by Time.
Near me he paused, and, growing garrulous
With memories of past years, when those around
Were animate, his creaking tongue ran on.

And ever told he some loud tale of mirth,
And ever, with a weird, uncanny sound,
His hollow laugh fell from his shrunken lips.
So long had he kept company with Death,
Brothered with speechless dust, and held for home
The house of Silence and the field of Sleep,
He seemed "the grim destroyer's" caricature, —
Death strayed abroad to prate with ghastly mirth
Of those his hand had clutched. But when he passed
To where a flower bloomed o'er a vine-wreathed grave, —
A tiny mound, — his quavering voice was hushed.
Down a deep furrow coursed the sudden tear;
"My all!" he said. His words were like a moan
At evenfall in gray November boughs.
Sad memories had made him once more man.

THE VIOLET BANK

ABOVE, a hoary hemlock flings
   Dense shade, and near, the bland day long,
The river-hasting brooklet sings
   In silvery undersong.

The airs that blow have pleasant hints
   Of mints and woody balsams pure;
On bough and bole and turf are tints
   That change and blend and lure.

THE HILLS OF SONG

And here, mosaicked in the moss —
  Blue as deep lakes in high noon's glow,
When not a ripple breathes across —
  The tender violets grow.

And here I love to set for Time
  A snare, to stay his feet that fly;
To fetter him with bonds of rhyme
  As he glides fleetly by.

Then to my eager lips I press
  The fruit Contentment's golden core;
The whole world, free from storm and stress,
  Is Arcady once more.

THE CRICKETS BY LAKE HURON

ALL through the afternoon, without reprieve,
  We marked the moaning of the inland main,
And then those cheery minstrels of the eve
  Resumed their jocund strain.

They flung it down the piny corridors,
  And through the cedar arches clear and far;
Wide Huron heard it, and her dusky shores,
  And heaven, star by star.

WILD PLUM

And, like a mother's hush-song to her child,
  It slowly softened as the night grew deep,
Until by happy dreams we were beguiled
    Upon the breast of sleep.

WILD PLUM

OVERHEAD is the hum
  Of the wind in the gloom
  Of the sentinel pines;
And below the wild plum,
    Where the slanting sun shines,
  Shows its snowy white bloom,
  Flings its subtle perfume
    On the breeze
    To the bees.

How they hover around,
  Tiny bandits and bold,
    Making thefts honey-sweet
With a murmurous sound!
    And the psyches they meet,
  Little atoms of gold,
  Join the frolic, and hold
    Jubilee
    Round the tree.

Where is Mab? where is Puck?
  Is that Ariel sings
    From the crest of yon bough

THE HILLS OF SONG

That no mortal should pluck?
O but list to it now!—
Revellings, rapturings;—
Then a glimmer of wings
And away
Like a ray.

How the bloom and the balm
And the bee and the bird,
In the depth of the wood,
To the heart bring a calm,
To the spirit seem good,
More than music or word!
Every fibre is stirred
By the hum,—
And the plum!

A BELL

HAD I the power
To cast a bell that should from some grand
tower,
At the first Christmas hour,
Outring,
And fling
A jubilant message wide,
The forgèd metals should be thus allied;—
No iron Pride,

A BELL

But soft Humility, and **rich-veined Hope**
Cleft from a sunny slope;
And there should be
White Charity,
And silvery Love, that knows not Doubt nor **Fear,**
To make the peal more clear;
And then to firmly fix the fine alloy,
There should be Joy!

IN ITALIA

THE SHEPHERD OF THE LIRO

ADOWN the Alpine vale our way we wended
  Toward fair Italia, wrapt in rosy haze;
And ever, when we thought the path had ended,
  New vistas opened to our wondering gaze.

Dark rocks lay strewn by ancient avalanches
  Where chestnuts clustered in a burry bower,
And often, o'er the autumn-ambered branches,
  A slender campanile thrust its tower.

The eyes we looked into were deep and dusky,
  Alive with laughter, yet with hints of pain;
The onward-luring air was warm and musky,
  Blown over Como from the Lombard plain.

And still alert for beauties unbeholden,
  Rounding a rock-ledge rearing bare and steep,
We saw, where stood a crumbling archway olden,
  An aged shepherd followed by his sheep.

His cloak hung crosswise from his stooping shoulder,
  While in his hand he held a sturdy crook;
His flock fast crowded over mound and bowlder,
  Nor did he guide them by a word or look.

And through the arch in happy-hearted frolic
  We watched them press behind him one by one,

THE HILLS OF SONG

Until our new Virgilian bucolic
　　Vanished as swiftly as the vanished sun.

Then violet shades crept down the winding valley
　　And hid the path our shepherd strayed along;
We heard the peasants, on their homeward rally,
　　Stirring the silence with a vintage song.

Erelong another roadway did we follow
　　Far into dreamland; there did we behold
The aged one, in some leaf-sheltered hollow,
　　Leading his flock benignly to the fold.

MEMORIES OF COMO

TRIUMPHANT Autumn sweeps from shore to shore,
　　And works swift magic with her wand of fire;
She fills the hollows of the hills once more
　　With amethyst, and like a golden lyre
　　The woodlands gleam, and quiver and suspire.

I listen, and the low harmonic sound
　　Quickens the happy past within my brain;
My spirit crosses with an ardent bound
　　The severing ocean, and I float again
　　On Como's tranquil breast that bears no stain.

Now buoyantly from vineyard-terraced heights
　　Are borne the soft and artless vintage airs;

NUOVA LUNA

Blent odors lend their attar-sweet delights,
   And by the lake's marge, on the water-stairs,
   I see the laughing lovers stand in pairs.

I view Varenna's milky-white cascade,
   And bright Bellaggio nestling 'neath a crown
Of laurel-woven, ilex-darkened shade;
   I mark o'er Lenno, looking grandly down,
   The pilgrim-haunted church of old renown.

Aye! and the mountains that uplift the soul
   Above the gross and earthly I behold;
And all the mighty shapes that mass and roll
   Through evanescent cloudland uncontrolled,
   And sunset skies miraculous with gold.

Dear to the heart are memories like these
   Of beauties seen upon some vanished day,
That, like the carven figures of a frieze
   In marble wrought, although the years decay,
   From fair perfection do not fade away.

NUOVA LUNA

" Blow up the trumpet in the new moon." — PSALMS.

THE Wind has fashioned him a harp to sound,
   Of cypress boughs, attuned to melody;
The sister wavelets wake the shores around
   With the sweet echo of their minstrelsy;
   Then give the lyre to me.

THE HILLS OF SONG

For yonder, o'er the mountains clearly shining,
    Companioned by one star,
    And riven by one violet cloud-bar,
  The new moon silvers in pale symmetry,
And song shall greet her ere her dim declining.

Like spectral opals in the emerald gloom,
    The frequent lights at far Tremezzo glow,
While titanesque the black peak-summits loom
    Along the sky-line in a rugged row.
  The waves are strange below,
Wan, wavering beams on tiny ripples glinting,
    Save where dense shadows fall
    Sheer from still wood or overtopping wall;
  There has begun night's unrecorded show
That takes no glamour from the new moon's tinting.

Soon will the mild and crescent-curving horn,
    A sparkling arc in darkling depths of air,
Swell to a golden globe, and then, at morn,
    Gleam like a ghost, in impotent despair
    That once her face was fair.
So rise, my song, before such change come o'er her!
    Youth is the meetest time
    For laughter, love, and ear-entrancing rhyme;
  Still youth's smooth brow doth beauty's garland wear,
The moon is young, and we would fain adore her.

THE PHANTOM GONDOLIER

Elsewhere our choric ecstasy were less,
    For inspiration would not lift our strain,
But here we grasp such perfect loveliness
    The full flood tide of bliss is almost pain
    To the enthrallèd brain,
And fancy spurns the earth for loftier soaring.
        'T is here, and only here,
        Yon cold and uninhabitable sphere
Warms the dull blood until it leaps amain,
And spurs the heart to passion's true outpouring.

Strive not to solve the riddle, — wherefore, why,
    The moonlight quickens here diviner things
Than under other arches of wide sky,
    Dulled with the dusk's sepulchral shadowings!
    Enough if it but brings
The rare uplifting, the supreme elation;
        O'er Crocione's crest,
        Its mirrored twin on Como's tranquil breast,
The new moon like an argent censer swings,
And song upsoars to voice our adoration.

THE PHANTOM GONDOLIER

IN Venice of the Doge's times,
    When Carnival was constant king,
When gallant nobles coupled rhymes
    And did their own gay minstreling,

THE HILLS OF SONG

There lived a gondolier whose grace
    Was like a charm we dream to see
In some remote, ethereal place,
    In some celestial Italy.

His oar had life; it swayed, it swept;
    It dipped as dips the bird in air.
Upon his olive face there slept
    A sunny look that made it fair.
And what a wondrous voice he had!
    When on the air its notes were borne,
The happy heard and grew more glad,
    And Sorrow's self forgot to mourn.

Rare bliss was his one little hour;
    A lovely princess deigned to throw
A rosebud from her latticed bower
    At twilight as he passed below.
And with the flower she flashed a smile
    That was to him a ray of light
Swift shot from some angelic isle
    Adown the drowning dusk of night.

Impassioned songs to her he sung
    When starry splendors filled the sky,
Till Scandal stirred its venom tongue,
    And fired a lover's jealousy.
A ruthless arbiter of fate,
    The vengeful noble lingered near,
And at the palace postern gate
    He slew the daring gondolier.

A VENETIAN SUNSET

And since that midnight hour of dread,
   In lawless mediæval days,
A spectral gondola has sped
   Adown the winding water-ways;
A graceful phantom plies the oar,
   And hurries on as if in fear;
A bodeful terror runs before
   Where hastes the ghostly gondolier.

Beheld but for a fleeting breath,
   Then suddenly the wraith is gone
With one swift shudder, as when death
   Steals in across the chill of dawn.
Who sees this phantom form may know
   That murder walks again abroad,
And that another face of woe
   Is staring dumbly up to God.

A VENETIAN SUNSET

ON the bright bosom of the broad lagoon
   Rocked by the tide we lay,
And watched the fading of the afternoon
   In golden calm away.

The water caught the fair faint hues of rose,
   Then flamed to ruby fire
That touched and lingered on the marble snows
   Of wall and dome and spire.

THE HILLS OF SONG

A graceful bark, with saffron sails outflung,
    Swept toward the ancient mart,
And poised a moment like a bird, and hung
    Full in the sunset's heart.

A dull gun boomed, and, as the echo ceased,
    O'er the low dunes afar,
Lambent and large from out the darkened east,
    Leaped night's first star.

ON A COPY OF THEOCRITUS

(Venice, 1493)

THEOCRITUS, we love thy song,
    Where thyme is sweet and meads are sunny;
Where shepherd swains and maidens throng,
    And bees Hyblean hoard their honey.

Since ancient Syracusan days
    It year by year has grown the sweeter;
For year by year life's opening ways
    Run more in prose and less in meter.

And than this quarto, vellum-clad,
    You could not wish a rarer setting;
Beholding, you must still be glad,
    If you behold without forgetting.

ON A COPY OF THEOCRITUS

Manutius was the Printer's name—
   (A *publisher* was then unheard of!)
A fellow of some worthy fame,
   If history we take the word of.

Think when its pages first were cut,
   And eager eyes above them hovered,
Our proudest dwelling was a hut—
   America was just discovered!

Then Venice was indeed a queen,
   And taught the tawny Turk to fear her;
Now has she lost her royal mien,
   And yet we could not hold her dearer.

Betwixt these covers there is bound
   A charm that needeth no completion;
A golden atmosphere is found
   At once Sicilian and Venetian.

So, while our plausive song we raise,
   And hail the bard whose name is famous,
Let us for once divide the bays,
   And to the Printer cry: *Laudamus!*

THE HILLS OF SONG

THE FALLING OF THE BURRS

WHEN russet-robèd Autumn reigns around,
    A tender chord within my memory stirs,
Hearing soft music on the leaf-strewn ground,
    The rhythmic falling of the chestnut burrs.

To me it means blue-skied, unfettered hours
    On Tuscan slopes above the figs and vines;
Below, red roofs and dazzling domes and towers,
    Beyond, in violet haze, the Apennines.

The cypresses in solemn conclave stand,
    Mourning the past with weird monotony;
A golden serpent, severing the land,
    Writhes Arno by toward Pisa and the sea.

The lizards bask, as indolent as I,
    In spaces where the unshattered sunbeams fall;
A tardy vintager goes stumbling by,
    Lilting a ditty, gaily bacchanal.

Such is the idyl — peaceful, dreamful, fair —
    Its only sober spot the somber firs,
Conjured by Autumn from the drowsy air
    With the down-dropping of the chestnut burrs.

A FLORENTINE GARDEN

A FLORENTINE GARDEN

How many summer suns have shone
   Upon this gem of garden closes,
With all its jars of céladon,
   And all its wealth of Tuscan **roses,**
On tablet or on page no hand
   With cunning letters has recorded;
Yet he who seeks this dreamy land
   Will find his wanderings rewarded.

Here citrons lean above the wall,
   And figs grow purple in September,
Here luscious-ripe the red plums fall —
   Each bursting globe a ruddy ember;
And here, inscribed upon a seat,
   With lichens gray, nicked, stained, and stony,
Twined in a love-knot, will he meet
   A "Paula" and a "Giorgione."

Who were they? That **we may not** know:
   Enough that 'neath the empyrean
They lived and loved, long, long ago,
   In days of splendor **Medicean.**
No doubt they saw the **hours** creep round
   The silver disc of yonder **dial,**
And 'neath the pleachèd laurels found
   A shelter safe from **all** espial.

THE HILLS OF SONG

In still word-pauses, fondly sweet —
　　A silence known to fools and sages —
Perchance he graved upon the seat
　　Their names, that have defied the ages;
Traced with his dagger, jewel-bright,
　　The characters we yet discover;
Then pledged himself her valiant knight,
　　And swore himself her faithful lover.

Perchance upon his speech she hung
　　With rapt regard, the radiant creature,
And answered with impassioned tongue,
　　Love limned on every flawless feature!
Mayhap they planned the future out,
　　As young troth-plighted people will do;
Of course he satisfied each doubt,
　　As castle-building suitors still do.

And were they wed with smiles and tears,
　　Here where all mortals toil and grope so?
And did they have full meed of years,
　　And pass to peaceful graves? We hope so!
And if, in some celestial sphere,
　　Unto their angel eyes should this come,
May they on two *now* loving here
　　Breathe down a tender "*Pax vobiscum!*"

THE BELLS OF FOSSOMBRONE

THE BELLS OF FOSSOMBRONE

UP the highlands, steep and stony,
    To the valley-wending throng,
Rang the bells of Fossombrone
    Silvery eve and matin song.

Rang they proud and rang they peerless,
    Rang they with ecstatic thrill;
And their music cheered the cheerless,
    Aye!—'t is said it healed the ill.

Then the Lord of Fano vaunted,
    "Great are we, and shall the dells
By rough mountain toilers haunted
    With their chimes outpeal our bells?"

So upon a morning moany,
    When the heavens were a-lower,
Stormed they into Fossombrone,
    Haled the bells from out the tower.

"When the Easter dawns," they boasted,
    "We will ring our triumph wide!"
And that night they blithely toasted
    Fano's power and Fano's pride.

Passed the year's young pilgrim daughters—
    Days both jubilant and lorn—

THE HILLS OF SONG

Till o'er Adria's waste of waters,
  Rose-like, flowered the Easter morn.

While the harbor shimmered steely,
  And the bloom of morning grew,
Toward the stately campanile
  Strode the ringers, two by two.

Soared a shout of acclamation
  Up as if some Titan spoke,
And with murmurous exultation
  Waited each the triumph stroke.

Gnarlèd muscles swelled with tension
  As the ringers strained and bowed;
Then a wave of apprehension
  Swept upon the gathered crowd;

For they saw the bells wide-swinging,
  Mouths agape as though to peal,
Yet they heard no sound down-ringing
  From the yawning throats of steel.

Cried one loudly, "We should rue us
  For the tale this Easter tells!
Hath not Jesus spoken to us
  In the silence of these bells?

"Back with them to Fossombrone!"
  Swiftly back their prize they bore,

THE BELLS OF FOSSOMBRONE

And beneath the highlands stony
 Found the bells their voice **once** more.

And the men of Fano, chided
 By the melody renewed,
Clasped the hands of those derided,
 Buried deep the olden feud.

Seaward from the mountain valley,
 Heralding the happier times,
Rang through grove and olive alley
 Fossombrone's peerless chimes.

EX ORIENTE

AL MAMOUN

BAGDAD'S palms looked tall in the tide
Of Tigris, tawny and swift and wide;
Bagdad's minarets gleamed and glowed
In the sun that burned in its blue abode;
Bagdad's life made rumble and jar
In booth and highway and bright bazaar;
Bagdad's monarch lolled in the dusk
Of the citron shade, 'mid the scent of musk,
And around him sat the makers of rhyme,
Come from many a distant clime;
For song by him was held as a boon,
    Al Mamoun,
  The son of the great Haroun.

From lands of cold and lands of the sun
He hearkened the poets, one by one,
Giving a portion of praise to each,
And a guerdon of gold with his pearls of speech;
Spreading a luscious banquet there
In the languid, richly-perfumed air;
Plucking from luxury's laden stem
The royal wealth of its fruit for them;
Bidding the soul of the grape be brought
To kindle the bosom to happy thought;
Speeding the amber afternoon,
    Al Mamoun,
  The son of the great Haroun.

THE HILLS OF SONG

And on through the starlit purple hours
The sound of song was heard in the bowers;
The zither and lute would blend and blur
And tangle with notes of the dulcimer;
And above and over and through it all
Would soar and swell, or would fail and fall
With the dreamful lull of the dying word,
An ecstasy voiced from the throat of a bird.
So, leashed by the love of song, would he,
Praising the poets and poesy,
Linger till night had neared its noon,
    Al Mamoun,
The son of the great Haroun.

With crumbling mosque and with toppling tomb
Have vanished Bagdad's beauty and bloom,
While a far, faint breath on the lips of fame
Is all we know of the monarch's name.
But rather to him than his mightier sire
O'er gulfs of time shall the song aspire;
For song to the lover of song is due,
Though centuries darken with rust, and strew
With mosses, the marble above his head.
And so, in the land of the happy dead,
May song still stir with its blissful boon
    Al Mamoun,
The son of the great Haroun.

DAWN IN THE DESERT

WHEN the first opal presage of the morn
    Quickened the east, the good Merwan arose,
And by his open tent door knelt and prayed.

Now in that pilgrim caravan was one
Whose heart was heavy with dumb doubts, whose eyes
Drew little balm from slumber. Up and down
Night-long he paced the avenues of sand
'Twixt tent and tent, and heard the jackals snarl,
The camels moan for water. This one came
On Merwan praying, and to him outcried —
(The tortured spirit bursting its sealed fount
As doth the brook on Damavend in spring),
"How knowest thou that any Allah is?"
Swift from the sand did Merwan lift his face,
Flung toward the east an arm of knotted bronze,
And said, as upward shot a shaft of gold,
"*Dost need a torch to show to thee the dawn?*"
Then prayed again.

                When on the desert's rim
In sudden, awful splendor stood the sun,
Through all that caravan there was no knee
But bowed to Allah.

THE HILLS OF SONG

KAROON, THE PILGRIM

NOON in Aleppo. For a little space
The babel died within the market-place,
And down the long bazaar the tread of feet
Knew soft cæsuras in its rhythmic beat.
Above mosaicked courts and house roofs dun
Kept fiery sovereignty the Syrian sun;
Without the town, where brown the hill lines rose,
The breeze scarce stirred the green pistachios,
And in the river garden slumbering
Were fount and bird and silvern zither string.

Karoon, the pilgrim, dozing by the door
Of Khan Wezir that threw cool shadow o'er
The nigh deserted highway, heard the din
Of hot Levantines quarreling within,
Roused, brushed the swarming flies, and set to lip
A few poor dates from out his scanty scrip,
Then grasped his staff and sought the distant star
Of light that glimmered through the dim bazaar.
The nets that hung o'er many an entrance there
Proclaimed the midday hour of rest and prayer;
But barter was not tongue-tied while the Greek
Or Syrian christian of his wares could speak.
Though ne'er in worldly ways had Karoon thrived,
Thought's hoarded honey in his brain was hived;

KAROON, THE PILGRIM

As radiant roses spring from darksome mold,
As seeming barren sands yield grains of gold,
As priceless pearls drop from the ragged shell,
From Karoon's lips a wealth of wisdom fell.
Past tiny stalls where gums and spices blent
To cloy the air with fumes of heavy scent,
Past wide divans, where, 'mid his curios,
The tarbooshed Moslem stole a brief repose,
Past slinking curs that scavengered the street,
Went Karoon, musing, through the noontide heat.
Raising his eyes, as branched the roofèd way,
He saw one brooding o'er a rare display
Of blue Bokharas, yellow Daghestans,
The choicest store of many caravans;
Hullal, the rich, men called him. Karoon stayed
His wandering steps, and man and wealth surveyed.
Deeply the merchant's face, despite his hoard,
With discontentment's arabesques was scored.
He met the pilgrim's eye with gaze unsure,
But cried to him, "What wouldst thou, O most poor?"
"Hold!" answered Karoon with unbended brow,
"Call him not poor who richer is than thou."
"Aha!" laughed Hullal, and "aha!" again,
"What monstrous fantasy beclouds thy brain?"
Calmly stood Karoon till the laughter died,
Then with the prophet tongue of truth replied,
"No empty mirage has my brain begot;
Mine is contentment, and thou hast it not."

THE HILLS OF SONG

Lightly he turned, and faded in the maze
Now thronged with men from Allah's house of
   praise,
While Hullal, sitting silent and apart,
Brooded and brooded with a heavy heart.

HASSAN'S TOMB

IN Hassan's heart there burned a lust for gold;
And growing overbold
With that consuming fire
That swept his soul as desert winds a lyre,
And wakened hot vibrations, in the cold
And silence-sealèd hours,
When in the sky the stars like golden flowers
Broke bud and bloomed, with stealthy foot he
   crept,
While all the palace slept,
To that vast vault, the kingdom's treasury,
Whereof, as trusted prince, he bore the key.

Then shone a Presence in a dream, and spoke;
And the Sultan awoke,
And girt himself, as though
He would go forth to battle with the foe.
And sandalled softly, so no footfall broke
Upon the midnight chill,
Through corridors and chambers dim and still
He glided like a spirit, till he came
Where, false to faith and fame,

THE ROSE OF FAYÛM

Stood Hassan, gloating with a greedy smile
O'er wealth that lay in many a gleaming pile.

The recreant stooped, with evil joy elate,
When, like avenging fate,
With eyes where fiery scorn
And lightnings of reproach alike were born,
The Sultan towered without the treasure gate.
Before the prince could stir,
Closed with a clang the massive barrier;
And, ere availing hand was on it laid,
Or plea for pardon made,
The tempter key that oped the door of doom
Had turned to bar the door of Hassan's tomb.

THE ROSE OF FAYÛM

COULD I pluck from the gardens of old
The fairest of flowers to behold,
And fashion a wreath for the shrine
Of the Muses, — the deathless, divine, —
A garland I 'd weave from the bloom
Of the redolent rose of Fayûm.

Still the hills with their sun-smitten crest
Tower barren and bold to the west,
Still slumbers the Lake of the Horns
'Neath the glory of luminous morns;
Still is attared the glow and the gloom
By the redolent rose of Fayûm.

THE HILLS OF SONG

Arsinoë's temples are prone,
And scarce is there stone above stone
Of the palace whose grandeur and girth
Was one of the wonders of earth;
But in triumph o'er time and the tomb
Springs the redolent rose of Fayûm.

The rose of to-day is a shoot,
Like the song, of a glorious root.
Side by side, till the ages shall close,
Go the love of the lute and the rose;
And my song I enlink with the bloom
Of the redolent rose of Fayûm.

THE DERVISH'S PRAYER

THE tyrant Yusef, crime and passion stained,
Upon the throne of gracious Haroun reigned.
Day after day, through busy Bagdad ran
Dark rumor ripples, — how this ruthless man
Goaded invention, so that he might see,
With every sunrise, some new agony.
Fear brooded o'er the city; then there came
Adown the breeze the murmur of a name,
And smiles again lit lip and eye, as though
The sun had pierced the midnight clouds of woe.
The blessèd dervish, he whose feet had traced
The path to Mecca o'er the weary waste

AT THE FUNERAL OF ABDALLAH

Devout each year for years a rounded score,
Was seen to pass along the streets once more.
"His prayers will save," the happy people cried,
"For ear to him hath Allah ne'er denied."

Scarce had the echo of their triumph slept,
When on their hope base Yusef's minions swept,
And bore him swift to be the tyrant's sport
Where high he sat, amid his cringing court.
"Slave," said the monarch, with a brutal stare,
"Lift me to Allah straight a goodly prayer,
Since it is noised through Bagdad broad that he
Will grant whatever may be asked by thee."

Thrice bowed the dervish Mecca-ward, the while
Around the throng ran changing sneer and smile;
Then rang his voice, as piercing as a fife
Above the clangorous din of battle strife,
"*I pray thee, Allah, take thou Yusef's life!*"

A form fell forward, writhing on the stone;
No more a tyrant ruled on Haroun's throne.

AT THE FUNERAL OF ABDALLAH

AT the funeral of Abdallah
    There were master mourners ten,
And they groaned and cried "Inshallah,"
    And they groaned and cried again.

THE HILLS OF SONG

They beat their palms with wailing
    Ere ever the round moon rose,
And loud, when her light was paling,
    Did the house-tops hear their woes.
As they swayed, about their faces
    Their locks were tossed and blown,
And the wide night's windy spaces
    Made answer, moan for moan.

O, the sounds that soared to Allah
At the funeral of Abdallah!

And not till the East gave token
    Of the bursting flower of dawn,
Was the lamentation broken
    By the mourners weak and wan.
Yet still did the sob of sorrow
    From the attared bower arise,
And the lorn day seemed to borrow
    From the night its brood of sighs.
Then the spicèd feast was eaten,
    And the solemn word was said,
And the doleful drum was beaten
    For the journey of the dead.

O, the sounds that deafened Allah
At the funeral of Abdallah!

THE VENGEANCE OF KAFUR

THE VENGEANCE OF KAFUR

FROM fair Damascus, as the day grew late,
Passed Kafur homeward through St. Thomas'
  gate
Betwixt the pleasure-gardens where he heard
Vie with the lute the twilight-wakened bird.
But song touched not his heavy heart, nor yet
The lovely lines of gold and violet,
A guerdon left by the departing sun
To grace the brow of Anti-Lebanon.
Upon his soul a crushing burden weighed,
And to his eyes the swiftly-gathering shade
Seemed but the presage of his doom to be, —
Death, and the triumph of his enemy.

"*One slain by slander*," cried he, with a laugh,
"Thus should the poets frame my epitaph,
Above whose mouldering dust it will be said,
'Blessèd be Allah that the hound is dead!'"
Outrang a rhythmic revel as he spake
From joyous bulbuls in the poplar brake,
Hailing the night's first blossom in the sky.
And now, with failing foot, he drew anigh
The orchard-garden where his home was hid
Pomegranate shade and jasmine bloom amid.

Despair mocked at him from the latticed gate
Where Love and Happiness had lain in wait

THE HILLS OF SONG

With tender greetings, and the lights within
Gleamed on the grave of Bliss that once had been.
Fair Hope, who daily poured into his ear
Her rainbow promises, gave way to Fear,
Who smote him blindly, leaving him to moan,
With bitter tears, before the gateway prone.

Soft seemed the wind in sympathy to grieve,
When lo! a sudden hand touched Kafur's sleeve,
And then a voice cried, echoing his name,
"Behold the proofs to put thy foe to shame!"
Upsprang the prostrate man, and while he stood
Gripping the proffered scrip in marvelhood,
He who had brought deliverance slipped from
    sight;
Thus Joy made instant day of Kafur's night.

"Allah is just," he said. . . . Then burning ire
With vengeance visions filled his brain like fire;
And to his bosom, anguish-torn but late,
Delirious with delight he hugged his hate.
"Revenge!" cried he; "why wait until the
    morn?
This night mine enemy shall know my scorn."
The stars looked down in wonder overhead,
As backward Kafur toward Damascus sped.

The wind, that erst had joined him in his grief,
Now whispered strangely to the walnut leaf;
Into the bird's song pleading notes had crept,
The happy fountains in the gardens wept,

THE VENGEANCE OF KAFUR

And e'en the river, with its restless roll,
Seemed calling "Pity" unto Kafur's soul.
"Allah," he cried, "O chasten thou my heart;
Move me to mercy, and a nobler part!"
Slow strode he on, the while a new-born grace
Softened the rigid outlines of his face,
Nor paused he till he struck, as ne'er before,
A ringing summons on his foeman's door.

His mantle half across his features thrown,
He won the spacious inner court unknown,
Where, on a deep divan, lay stretched his foe,
Sipping his sherbet cool with Hermon snow;
Who, when he looked on Kafur, hurled his hate
Upon him, wrathful and infuriate,
Bidding him swift begone, and think to feel
A judge's sentence and a jailer's steel.

"Hark ye!" cried Kafur, at this burst of rage
Holding aloft a rollèd parchment page;
"Prayers and not threats were more to thy behoof;
Thine is the danger, see! I hold the proof.
Should I seek out the Caliph in his bower
To-morrow when the mid-muezzin hour
Has passed, and lay before his eyes this scrip,
Silence would seal forevermore thy lip.
Aye! quail and cringe and crook the supple knee,
And beg thy life of me, thine enemy,
Whom thou, a moment since, didst doom to death.
I will not breathe suspicion's lightest breath

THE HILLS OF SONG

Against thy vaunted fame: and even though
Before all men thou 'st sworn thyself my foe,
And pledged thyself wrongly to wreak on me
Thy utmost power of mortal injury,
In spite of this, should I be first to die
And win the bowers of the blest on high,
Beside the golden gate of paradise
Thee will I wait with ever-watchful eyes,
Ready to plead forgiveness for thy sin,
If thou shouldst come, and shouldst not enter in.
Should Allah hear my plea, how sweet! how sweet!
For then would Kafur's vengeance be complete."

THE ARAB'S HORSE

IN the heart of the wild Hauran
   The Druse and the Arab met,
And man against maddened man
   In a frenzied fight was set.

Then the Druses' star grew bright,
   And the star of the Arabs pale,
And was drowned in the battle's night
   Like a tempest-drownèd sail.

From the fatal circle free
   Broke one on his loyal steed;—
The chief of the Arabs he,
   His horse of the Nedjid breed.

THE ARAB'S HORSE

A laugh that swelled to a cry,
   A shake of the bridle rein,
And lo! as a swift doth fly
   He skimmed o'er the pathless plain.

Like hawks on the quarry's track
   Did the Druses race behind,
While the fugitive shouted back
   His defiance down the wind.

And ever away he drew,
   And ever and ever away,
Though the foiled pursuers flew
   Like the buck ere he turn at bay.

Then, "Stay thee!" the foremost cried,
   "May Allah strike me a corse
If a shadow of harm betide
   One who rides such a noble horse."

Again in the wild Hauran
   Have the Druse and the Arab met;
Forgotten the blood that ran
   As the desert's sons forget.

They have kissed the face of the steed,
   They have bathed its feet and flanks;
For his crowning gift to his children's need
   They have given Allah thanks.

THE HILLS OF SONG

IN A BAZAAR

WITHOUT, the ways in sunlight swim,
But here the day is dusk and dim;
Without, discordant cries resound,
But here cool quietude is found.
Wrapt in this scented twilight lie
Treasures that charm the alien eye; —
Rugs, soft as sleep to weary lids;
Rings, ancient as the pyramids,
With sacred scarabs set therein;
Blades, scintillant and curved and thin;
Long ink-horns, carved with scroll and swirl;
Divans, inwrought with mother-pearl,
And many another precious thing
To stir the mind's imagining.

Thou mayest buy, and yet beware
The merchant with his luring snare,
Who, while his bland words promise well,
Is, like the sphinx, inscrutable.
Let not thine eyes betray desire,
Lest he should note their eager fire;
Have caution warder of thy lip,
Lest through the gate thy wish should slip;
Strive, if may be, to match his mood
Who 'mid his treasures seems to brood
Indifferent, and calm of brow,
If not a coin his palm endow;

IN A BAZAAR

But know a cunning must be met
That plummet never sounded yet.

Should fabric from a Bagdad loom
For thee make radiant the gloom,
And conjure swift a vision fair, —
Its gloss above the gold-brown hair
Of one whose face illumes the day
In happy home-land far away, —
Lead thou to it with fine device,
And curious questioning of price
On broidery and jewelled blade,
On bits of amber and of jade ;
Then, if thy suit thou subtly press,
The silken prize thou may'st possess,
And, in the halcyon future, bring
To love an Orient offering.

THE HILLS OF SONG

CHRISTMAS AT MARSABA *

The monks CONSTANTINE *and* PAUL *meet upon the monastery terrace above the gorge of the Brook Kedron.*

CONSTANTINE—
    A merry Christmas, brother, though, forsooth,
    Were we elsewhere the day were merrier.
PAUL—
    Merry's a word my weary heart knows not.
CONSTANTINE—
    Bethink you then of dinner — a fat kid
    Well stuffed, and herbs from Artas gardens brought,
    And rice deep-isled in juice of apricots,
    A Christmas feast for any Bishop fit,—
    Say you not so?
PAUL—
              Aye! truly, though you mock me.
CONSTANTINE—
    Nay, by Saint Sabas, in good faith I spake.
    When we are better friends you will not doubt
    The true and trusty lip of Constantine.
    Came you last night?

---

* Marsaba — a Greek monastery in the wilderness of Judea overlooking the rocky gorge of the Kedron. It takes its name from a celebrated anchorite, Sabas, who lived in the fifth century. Refractory monks are sometimes confined here.

CHRISTMAS AT MARSABA

PAUL —
                                 At middle vesper hour.
The crazy bell that hangs from yon low dome
Shook its cracked sides and clamored an alarm,
While eager pilgrims at the outer gate
Shouted till Kedron's rocks gave answer back.
Methinks your knees were scarce so chaste in prayer
That such unwonted tumult moved you not.

CONSTANTINE —
Brother, our prayers here are not empty breath.

PAUL —
I know Marsaba.

CONSTANTINE [*aside*] —
                        And good cause, mayhap . . .
The noisy pilgrims were your comrades, then —
The men who wended Jordan-ward at dawn,
Singing their slow way through the wilderness ?
Went not your heart forth with them on their way ?
Alas ! the cruel manacles of fate
Close hold you here. Mine eyes have told my brain
That lonely Petra, or the wildest spot
On Sinai's slopes, or in hot Araby,
Hath greater charm for you than these gray walls.

PAUL —
Your eyes are keen, yet no more keen than mine

THE HILLS OF SONG

    That counsel me our dear desires are twin;
    And now your brow makes sign affirmative.
CONSTANTINE —
    Dost not the lifted brow mean "nay" in
        Greece?
PAUL —
    How knew you, brother, that Greece fathered
        me?
CONSTANTINE —
    Aha! 't is so, then! Faith, that paunch of
        yours,
    So like the casks your dim wine-cellars hold,
    As much as said you were no Syrian.
    Soft — soft — a jest! — but, in all earnestness,
    Ere six months pass, you'll gird your loins
        like mine.
PAUL —
    I have no stomach for such prophecy.
CONSTANTINE —
    Most bravely answered!
                      But rest here awhile
    Upon this wide, smooth seat, and let me hear
    Why you have come to grim Marsaba's walls.
PAUL —
    Will you, in turn, if I do thus confide,
    Relate the wherefore of your coming, too?
CONSTANTINE —
    Aye! you shall hear.
PAUL —
                  My brief and broken tale —
    I pray you, hold it not beyond belief! —

CHRISTMAS AT MARSABA

Is this. In youth I took the holy vows,
And after years of ministration, deep
In the wild quiet of Thessalian dales,
I came to dwell 'neath that white-hearted
   mount
Whose crest looks down on level Marathon.
A lovely spot! The silvery poplars weave
In early spring a breezy web of shade —
A boon in summer hours — and nigh, a fount
Fills night and day with dulcet melody.
One autumn eve, not many months agone,
I wandered forth along a winding way
That led me mountain-ward, and near the path
I saw a youth, footsore and faint and wan
From arduous climbing, who besought my aid.
When I had propped his steps and found him
   food,
Into the murky night he needs must plunge,
Despite my proffered hospitality.
Till dawn the wind made wail, and in my
   dreams
Red landscapes reeled, and wraiths with blood-
   shot eyes
Mocked merciless. Then broke the pallid
   day,
And soon around the monastery gates
There rose a clamor. In the heat of haste
I joined the press of peasants. Following one
To where the roadway elbowed, stark in death
My hapless youthful guest before me lay.
Then dizzy fear gripped sudden at my heart,

THE HILLS OF SONG

For by his side, encrimsoned with his blood,
I saw the knotted staff I late had lost.
Slow wore the days, while black suspicion grew,
Till from the church's head a mandate came
That damned with banishment my innocence.
Thus was I made the butt of circumstance
Who ne'er had raised a life-destroying hand
Against the meanest thing God set on earth.

CONSTANTINE —
A woful tale, if e'er I hearkened one.

PAUL —
A true one, too, by all men reverence!
Believe you not? That flitting smile of scorn
Breeds angry doubt in my impatient breast.
Do not deride me, lest endurance fail!

CONSTANTINE —
I can but think how good Saint Sabas' beast,
The lion that he met in yonder cave,
And lived with long, had made a meal of you.

PAUL —
Methinks at last I see you as you are —
The sneering knave beneath the monk's white gown.
Now, hearken me! if you do think I'll brook
Your fleering insults, you do greatly err.

CONSTANTINE —
One's food for mirth in these Judean wilds
Is sadly small. You prove a tempting bit.

PAUL —
By Olivet, and by the Holy Cross,

CHRISTMAS AT MARSABA

    That jeering tongue of yours shall feel a vise,
    And cease its mocking. [*Springs upon him.*]
                    Never hand of man
    Closed round a clammier, baser throat than
      this.
CONSTANTINE —
    Gentle my brother, loose your heavy clutch
    That I may beg forgiveness. Saints! I choke;
    You force a jest too far.
PAUL —   A jest, indeed!
CONSTANTINE [*mutters*] —
    How slight a feint deludes the easy fool!
    A sudden hate grows hot within my heart;
    Let me but press him toward the rail of stone,
    One grip at his soft hands, a push, and then —
PAUL —
    What mean you, wretch?
               My God, be merciful! [*Falls.*]
CONSTANTINE —
    When had the jackals such a Christmas feast
    As this to-day, since paynim Persian hordes
    Dyed Kedron's craggy bed with tides of
      blood?
    By chance, to-morrow I will see his bones
    As they lie white along the rocks below —
    Should no one mark ere then — and point
      them out
    With horrified amazement. Martyrdom
    In yonder hillside cave claims many a skull;
    There his shall rest. He should be satisfied
    To find a place among such worthy men.

There will be mass, and many candles burned,
And *aves* said.   [*A bell sounds.*]
                      But, hark ! — *I must to prayers!*

FROM AN EASTERN ORIEL

WITH longing that is almost pain
    I eastward turn my face again,
And see the mounting morning glow
Cast beckoning beams across the snow.
The walls of circumstance are high,
And duty's gyves forbid me fly;
But neither wall nor gyve can bind
The Orient journeys of my mind.

I close my eyes, and lo! the lote
Not lighter lies than does my boat
Upon the languid waters born
Where Kilimandjaro cleaves the morn.
I mount a strange craft, bridle-manned,
And sail across a sea of sand,
Along whose rim, by fierce light frayed,
The mirage-palm trees form and fade.

In fragrant citron gardens green,
A dusky, dreamful Damascene,
I while luxurious hours away
O'er sherbet and a nargileh.
I watch the rose of sunset pale
Above the downcast shrines of Baal,

FROM AN EASTERN ORIEL

And mark forth-flower night's earliest star
Where Lebanon's hoar cedars are.

Then fate may fence me round, and fact
My clear horizon-line contract;
Howe'er **this be,** I'll not repine
If memory's **magic** key be mine
To turn, while ways without **are frore,**
And open swing the golden door.

MADRIGALS

VIVE LA BAGATELLE

(*"Swift's Cheerful Creed."*)

A BUMPER to the jolly Dean
   Who, in " Augustan " times,
Made merriment for fat and lean
   In jocund prose and rhymes !
Ah, but he drove a pranksome quill !
   With quips he wove a spell ;
His creed — he cried it with a will —
   Was "*Vive la bagatelle !*"

Oh, there were reckless jesters then !
   And when a man was hit,
He quick returned the stroke again
   With trenchant blade of wit.
'T was parry, thrust, and counter-thrust
   That round the board befell ;
They quaffed the wine and crunched the crust
   With "*Vive la bagatelle !*"

How rang the genial laugh of Gay
   At Pope's defiant ire !
How Parnell's sallies brought in play
   The rapier wit of Prior !
And how o'er all the banter's shift —
   The laughter's fall and swell —
Upleaped the great guffaw of Swift,
   With "*Vive la bagatelle !*"

THE HILLS OF SONG

O moralist, frown not so dark,
    Purse not thy lip severe;
'T will warm the heart if ye but **hark**
    The mirth **of** "yester year."
To-day we wear too grave a face;
    We slave, — we buy and sell;
Forget awhile mad Mammon's race
    In "*Vive la bagatelle!*"

THE SWEET O' THE YEAR

(A Song for Any Season.)

ONCE I heard a piper playing
    Notes that blissful ardors fanned;
All the world had gone a-Maying
    Up and down the flowery land.
"Tell me," said I, "piper merry,
    Why you blow such tuneful cheer!
Far and near, by ford and ferry,
    Is it now 'the sweet o' the year'?"
    Gracious answer was my guerdon,
    And his ditty bore this burden: —
Crimson cherry, holly berry, rod-of-gold, or jonquil-spear!
Love-time! Love-time! Then's "the sweet o' the year."

When the meads were ripe for mowing,
    Underneath the ancient stars

THE SWEET O' THE YEAR

Stood a songful shepherd, sowing
   Night with music's rapture-bars.
"Singer," cried I, "buoyant-hearted,
   Bounteous harvest draweth near,
But has joy from sorrow parted,—
   Is it now 'the sweet o' the year'?"
     Still his **voice rang,** upward soaring
     With its rhythmical outpouring:—
Crimson cherry, holly berry, rod-of-gold, or jonquil-spear!
Love-time! Love-time! Then's "the sweet o' the year."

When the linden leaves were **yellow,**
   From the orchard welled **a strain**
Where a lilting lad with mellow
   Apples piled the waiting wain.
Eagerly I hailed him, thinking
   "Aye" on answering "aye" to hear,—
"Why such jocund rhymes art linking?
   Is it now 'the sweet o' the year'?"
     Straight into a chorus broke **he,**
     And in mounting measure spoke he:
*Crimson cherry, holly berry, rod-of-gold, or **jonquil-spear!***
Love-time! Love-time! Then's "the sweet o' the year."

When the hills were silver-sided,
   And the **skies were steely cold,**

THE HILLS OF SONG

Chance my wandering footsteps guided
  To a forest gray and old.
There a lusty-voicèd woodman
  Swung his axe, and carolled clear;
"Ho!" I called, "my gay, my good man,
  Is it now 'the sweet o' the year'?"
    Came his rapturous replying,
    Rising, falling, swelling, dying:—
Crimson cherry, holly berry, rod-of-gold, or jonquil-spear!
Love-time! Love-time! Then's "the sweet o' the year."

A CAVALIER'S VALENTINE

(*1644*)

THE sky was like a mountain mere,
  The lilac buds were brown,
What time a war-worn cavalier
  Rode into Taunton-town.
He sighed and shook his head forlorn;
  "A sorry lot is mine,"
He said, "who have this merry morn
  Pale Want for Valentine."

His eyes, like heather-bells at dawn,
  Were blue and brave and bold;
Against his cheeks, now wan and drawn,
  His love-locks tossed their gold.

WITH SOME WHITE HYACINTHS

And as he rode, beyond a wall
   With ivy overrun,
His glance upon a maid did fall,
   A-sewing in the sun.

As sweet was she as wilding thyme,
   A boon, a bliss, a grace:
It made the heart blood beat in rhyme
   To look upon her face.
He bowed him low in courtesy,
   To her deep marvelling;
"Fair Mistress Puritan," said he,
   "It is a forward spring."

As when the sea-shell flush of morn
   Throws night in rose eclipse,
So sunshine smiles, that instant born,
   Brought brightness to her lips;
Her voice was modest, yet, forsooth,
   It had a roguish ring;
"*You*, sir, of all should know that truth—
   It *is* a forward spring!"

WITH SOME WHITE HYACINTHS IN WINTER

GO to my sweet for me, flowers, and repeat for me
   All that my heart would cry out o'er the waste to her.

THE HILLS OF SONG

Pause in the valley not ; on the hill dally not ;
  Winged with my love and my longing, oh,
    haste to her !

Ring your white bells for her !—(not any knells
    for her !)—
  Chimes that are fragrant and rich in their rarity.
Bid her be leal to me, loyal as steel to me ;
  Bid her have faith in me ; bid her have charity !

INGLE SONG

OVERHEAD the gray clouds go,
  And the air is thick with snow ;
In the bitter icy blur
Spectrally the trees confer ;
And the sad wind seems to cry,
  To a wild and woful tune,
Sobbing down the shrouded sky,
  " O for joy again, and June ! "

  Heart belovèd, have no fear !
  Thine and mine is June-day cheer :
  For, though moans the sullen storm,
  Love shall keep our ingle warm.

Now the shivering twilight brings
Raven night, with brooding wings ;
Not a single star of hope
Flowers on heaven's gloomy slope ;

BE YE IN LOVE WITH APRIL-TIDE

And adown the wailing blast,
   To the same wild, woful tune,
Still that sobbing cry is cast —
   "O for joy again, and June!"

Yet, beloved, shrink not thus!
All the year is June for us,
Since, though moans the sullen storm,
Love still keeps our ingle warm.

BE YE IN LOVE WITH APRIL-TIDE

BE ye in love with April-tide?
   I' faith, in love am I!
For now 't is sun, and now 't is shower,
And now 't is frost, and now 't is flower,
And now 't is Laura laughing-eyed,
   And now 't is Laura shy.

Ye doubtful days, O slower glide!
   Still smile and frown, O sky!
Some beauty unforeseen I trace
   In every change of Laura's face; —
Be ye in love with April-tide?
   I' faith, in love am I!

THE HILLS OF SONG

A SPRING GLEE

THE rathe hepatica has spread
    A carpet for the feet of spring;
The blithe wake-robin lifts its head,
    The violet is bourgeoning.
And through the bud-brown forest bowers
    Trips one whose face 't is joy to see;
Her presence, more than all the flowers,
    Brings spring to me.

Then it's, O my heart, be light!
    And it's, O my lip, be gay!
In Sylvia's eyes is April,
    And in her smile is May.

In clearings shows the mandrake shoot,
    The cowslips hide the marsh's mire;
The blue-flag quickens at the root,
    And brier stems are flushed with fire.
All nature feels the vernal thrill,
    And bids the thraldom broken be,
But love it is whose tender will
    Brings spring to me.

Then it's, O my heart, be light!
    And it's, O my lip, be gay!
In Sylvia's eyes is April,
    And in her smile is May.

ROSES OF JUNE

ROSES OF JUNE

TWINE not for me those crimson queens of bloom
   That make Damascus gardens a delight;
Wreathe not the royal blossoms that perfume
   The star-bright spaces of Egyptian night;

Nor yet the Italian rose that garlanded
   The brow of Petrarch's Laura; nor the flowers
That warred in merry England — white and red —
   Till Joy's head drooped and Sorrow knelled the hours.

But pluck from yonder hedgerow in the field —
   As pure as sweet, as delicate as fair —
The dearest boon the days of June-time yield,
   The pale wild rose that Sylvia loves to wear.

STRAWBERRIES

AGAIN the year is at the prime
   With flush of rose and cuckoo-croon;
Care doffs his wrinkled air, and Time
   Foots to a gamesome tune.
      So, ho! my lads, an' if you will
      But follow underneath the hill,
         It's strawberries! strawberries!
      You shall feast, and have your fill.

THE HILLS OF SONG

The elder clusters promise wine
  Where dips the path along the lane;
The early lowing of the kine
  Floats in a far refrain;
     You will forget to dream indeed
     Of fruit that Georgian loam-lands breed
       In strawberries! strawberries!
    That wait for us in Martin's mead.

Then haste, before the sun be high,
  And, haply, catch the morning star;
For, ere the cups of dew be dry,
  The berries sweetest are.
     And if, perchance, a rustic lass
     In merriment a-milking pass,
       It's strawberries! strawberries!
    On her lips as in the grass.

A SUMMER SONG

AH! whither, sweet one, art thou fled —
  My heart of May?
In vain pursuing I am led
  A weary way.

The brook is dry; its silver throat
  Rills song no more;
And not a linnet lifts a note
  Along the shore.

WILD THYME

Wilt thou return ? — I ask the night,
　　I ask the morn.
The doubt that wounds the old delight
　　Is like a thorn.

Oh, come !　I lean my eager ear
　　For laughter's ring ;
Bring back the love-light cool and clear —
　　Bring back my Spring !

WILD THYME

RING, ring, my rhyme,
　　The praises of wild thyme !
Wild thyme that grows
Beside the green hedgerows,
Or on gray wall
With scent ambrosial.

Above the meres
Where every fern-slope hears
The echoes mock,
And shout from rock to rock,
In nook and chink
It shows its modest pink.

Whence did it win
The fragrance lurking in
Its tiny heart ?
Not such hath any mart

THE HILLS OF SONG

In Occident,
Or attared Orient.

Her worshipper,
Wild thyme I bring to her;
Upon her breast
It shall know perfect rest.
To love — thus fate
Bids it be consecrate !

THE EVEN-SONG

NOW the west is warm, and now
Plaintive is the bird on bough ;
Now the primrose shyly opes,
   Watching for its sister stars,
And the flocks adown the slopes
   Loiter toward the pasture bars.
Now that thickening shadows throng,
This shall be our even-song :

> *Unto youth, with night above,*
> *Welcome are the wings of love ;*
> *Unto age, when shades grow deep,*
> *Welcome are the wings of sleep.*

Now the brooding ear receives
Little laughters from the leaves ;
Now the breeze is like a breath
   Over seas from shores of spice,

A PERFECT DAY

And the heart within us saith,
  "We are nigh to paradise."
Now that discord were a wrong,
This shall be our even-song:

    Unto age, when shades grow deep,
    Welcome are the wings of sleep;
    Unto youth, with night above,
    Welcome are the wings of love.

A PERFECT DAY

BLAND air, and leagues of immemorial blue;
No subtlest hint of whitening rime or cold;
A revel of rich color, hue on hue,
  From radiant crimson to soft shades of gold.

A vagueness in the undulant hill-line,
  The flutter of a bird's south-soaring wing,
Æolian harmonies in groves of pine,
  And glad brook-laughter like the mirth of spring.

A sense of gracious calm afar and near,
  And yet a something wanting, — one fine ray
For consummation. Love, were you but here,
  Then were the day indeed a perfect day.

THE HILLS OF SONG

THE BOWERS OF PARADISE

O TRAVELER, who hast wandered far
　'Neath southern sun and northern star,
Say where the fairest regions are !

Friend, underneath whatever skies
Love looks in love-returning eyes,
There are the bowers of paradise.

HOLLY SONG

CARE is but a broken bubble,
　Trill the carol, troll the catch ;
Sooth, we 'll cry, " A truce to trouble ! "
Mirth and mistletoe shall match.

　　Happy folly! we'll be jolly!
　　　Who'd be melancholy now?
　　With a "Hey, the holly! Ho, the holly!"
　　Polly bangs the holly bough.

Laughter lurking in the eye, sir,
　Pleasure foots it frisk and free.
He who frowns or looks awry, sir,
　Faith, a witless wight is he !

HOLLY SONG

Merry folly! what a volley
  Greets the banging of the bough!
With a " Hey, the holly! Ho, the holly!"
  Who'd be melancholy now?

THE FIRST EDITION OF THIS BOOK CONSISTS OF FIVE HUNDRED COPIES WITH FIFTY ADDITIONAL COPIES ON HAND-MADE PAPER PRINTED DURING NOVEMBER 1895 BY THE EVERETT PRESS BOSTON.

www.ingramcontent.com/pod-product-compliance
Lightning Source LLC
Chambersburg PA
CBHW032239080426
42735CB00008B/921